STEP-BY-STEP
Paper Fun for Kids

STEP-BY-STEP
Paper Fun for Kids

Marion Elliot

Photography by James Duncan

SMITHMARK

PUBLISHER'S NOTE

*Crafts and hobbies are great fun to learn and can fill many
rewarding hours of leisure time, but some general points should be
remembered for safety and care of the environment.*

● *Always use non-toxic materials, for example paints, glues and
varnishes. If this is not possible, always use materials in a
well-ventilated area and always follow manufacturers'
instructions.*

● *Craft knives, needles, scissors and all sharp instruments should
be used with care. Always use a cutting board or matt to avoid
damage to household surfaces (it is also safer to cut onto a firm,
non-slip surface).*

● *Protect surfaces from paint, glue and varnish splashes by laying
down old newspapers, plastic sheeting or an old sheet.*

SOME USEFUL TERMS

US	UK
cellophane tape	*sticky tape*
construction paper	*cartridge paper*
posterboard	*card*
string	*cord*
white glue	*PVA glue*

To George, Annie and Jessica

© Anness Publishing Limited 1994

This edition published in 1994 by
SMITHMARK Publishers Inc.
16 East 32nd Street
New York
NY 10016

SMITHMARK books are available for bulk purchase for sales
promotion and for premium use. For details write or call
the Manager of Special Sales, SMITHMARK Publishers Inc.
16 East 32nd Street, New York, NY, 10016; (212) 532–6600.

ISBN 0 8317 7844 X

Produced by Anness Published Limited
1 Boundary Row
London SE1 8HP

Editorial Director: Joanna Lorenz
Series Editor: Lindsay Porter
Designer: Peter Laws
Jacket Designer: Peter Butler
Photographer: James Duncan

Printed and bound in Italy by Graphicom S.r.l., Vincenza

CONTENTS

Introduction   **6**

TECHNIQUES   **12**

TEMPLATES   **18**

PAPER DECORATIONS   **22**

PAPER PROJECTS   **42**

PAPER GIFTS   **70**

Index   **96**

INTRODUCTION

We all use paper every day. Newspapers tell us what is happening in the world; letters bring us news from friends; paper wraps our parcels and fills our books; cardboard protects our food and decorative paper covers our walls. Paper is all around us and life would be very difficult without it.

Paper may be used in other ways too, and this book shows you how to create all kinds of fun objects to use as decoration or to give to your friends. All the projects in this book use paper in its many varieties, and each one shows you what materials to use and how it's done. Some of the projects can be made all by yourself, and others may need an adult's help, but you're sure to want to try them all. Remember, you don't have to copy the projects exactly – you can make up your own items using some of the ideas you've learned. This book is only the beginning, and all you need is paper, a little patience and your imagination.

Different Types of Paper

Coloured paper
Lightweight coloured paper is used for projects that involve folding, decoupage and collage amongst other techniques. Medium-weight and heavy paper are suitable for scoring, cutting, printing and folding.

Corrugated cardboard
This is perfect for making armatures for papier-mâché projects. It comes in a variety of thicknesses. Use clean, uncreased board for best results. Good sources of cardboard are discarded computer and TV boxes.

Crêpe paper
A very dry-textured, rather stretchy paper, this comes in a wide range of colours and is generally used for wrapping and sculptural effects.

Decorative corrugated card (posterboard)
Corrugated card is less heavy than corrugated cardboard used in the papier-mâché projects. It comes in various colours and its corrugations are used as a decorative feature.

Doll's house paper
Interesting papers are available for decorating doll's houses. They come in a variety of patterns including brick, stone, tile and wood and are very useful for general decorative work.

Graph paper
This is useful for scaling-up templates that are given in a reduced size.

Handmade paper
Handmade paper is made in a two-part frame called a deckle and mould. All sorts of things including seeds, plants, hair, glitter, wool, very fine thread and food colouring can be added to the pulp to make interesting textures in the paper.

Origami paper
This highly decorated, very colourful thin paper comes ready-cut into squares. It is used for making origami projects, but is also good for general decorative work and collage.

Paper ribbon
This comes tightly rolled and is unfurled to give a wide crinkly ribbon which is good for stiff bows.

Recycled paper
Now widely available, machine-made recycled paper has a texture rather like blotting paper and is very porous. It generally has an attractive speckled surface owing to the various types of paper in the pulp.

Stencil card (cardboard)
This is usually waxed to prevent it absorbing water from paint and disintegrating. Transparent plastic stencil film is also available.

Thin card (posterboard)
This comes in a range of colours and is perfect for making items such as hats and masks that will be handled frequently.

Tissue paper
Tissue paper is a very fine, thin paper that appears translucent when held to the light. It can be used in many projects and is especially good for stained-glass effects.

Tracing paper
This comes in several thicknesses and can be bought in large single sheets or in pads.

doll's house paper

tissue paper

graph paper

tracing paper

stencil card
(cardboard)

coloured paper

thin card
(posterboard)

handmade
paper

corrugated cardboard

decorative corrugated
card (posterboard)

origami paper

crêpe paper

recycled paper

paper ribbon

Materials and Equipment

Coloured pencils and crayons
These must be non-toxic. They come in a huge variety of colours and are useful for decorating projects.

Cotton string
Cotton string comes in a variety of colours and is useful for binding pages together, stringing beads and making picture hangers.

Eye pins
These are small metal pins with a loop at one end. They are used mostly in jewellery to join items such as earrings together. They can be bought from specialist craft and hobby shops.

Hole punch
Use with adult supervision to make holes in paper for decoration or practical purposes.

Household sponge
This can be cut into small squares and used to apply paint with or without stencils.

Ink pad
Use an ink pad with non-toxic ink to stamp stationery and other projects.

Masking tape
Masking tape is cream-coloured paper tape that can be removed once it has been stuck down. It is particularly useful for keeping joints in position whilst glue dries.

Paintbrushes
Paintbrushes in a variety of thicknesses are used for applying glue and paint.

Paints
These must be non-toxic. Paints are used in several projects, especially for decorating papier-mâché.

Paper clips
Paper clips are very useful for holding small pieces of paper together while you are working on a project.

Paper fasteners
These are split metal pins that open out to hold pieces of paper together. They should only be used under adult supervision.

Paper glue
This must be non-toxic. Paper glue comes in a variety of formats. Perhaps the easiest to use is the solid stick of glue.

PVA (white) glue
This must be non-toxic.

Undiluted PVA glue is very useful for sticking heavy cardboard. Diluted, it can be used for papier-mâché.

Rubber cutting mat
These mats are non-slip and protect work surfaces when cutting paper and card.

Ruler
Use for measuring and drawing straight lines.

Scissors
These should be of the type made specially for children with rounded blades.

Sequins
Sequins in various shapes and sizes make very good decorations.

Stapler and staples
These should be used under adult supervision. Staples are very useful for holding paper together, especially joints in fairly thick papers and cards.

Sticky tape
Clear sticky tape is good for sticking paper, cord and card.

Strong glue
This must be non-toxic and solvent-free. Strong glue is sometimes used to fix heavyweight papers.

household sponge

masking tape

sticky tape

ink pad

coloured
pencils

cotton string

rubber
cutting
mat

paper clips

crayons

strong glue

eraser

eye pins

ruler

darning elastic

stapler

sequins

scissors

staples

paper glue

pencil sharpener

sequins

paintbrushes

paper fasteners

hole punch

paints

PVA (white) glue

TECHNIQUES

Folding

Paper can be folded in a variety of ways to great effect. One of the simplest methods is to fold a sheet of paper into equal sections rather like a concertina. You can hang up the finished design as a decoration.

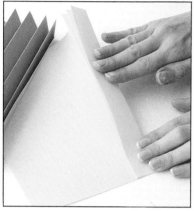

1 Fold two sheets of paper in contrasting colours into sections approximately 2.5 cm (1 in) wide.

2 Fold each piece of paper in the middle to make a semi-circle. Under adult supervision, fix the ends of the paper together with a staple.

3 Under adult supervision, join the two semi-circles together at the outside edges with staples to form a circle.

Scoring

Scoring is a method of creating fold lines in paper so that it can be creased to appear three-dimensional. Some very elaborate effects can be achieved once the technique has been mastered. Score lines can be made with a pair of scissors, but the blades should *always* be kept *closed*, and you should do it under adult supervision.

1 Draw the outline of your shape on heavy paper or lightweight card (posterboard). Add the fold line.

2 Carefully cut out the shape. Using a pair of closed, round-ended scissors, gently score along the fold line to produce an indentation.

3 Gently fold the shape along the score line. Lightly re-score the line if it doesn't fold easily.

12

Curling

Thin strips of lightweight paper can be pulled with a pencil to create gentle curls. The curls are especially good for making false beards, moustaches, hair, fur effects and so on.

1 Cut thin strips of paper approximately 1 cm (⅜ in) wide.

2 Holding a strip of paper in one hand, pull a pencil down its length several times. Don't pull too hard or you'll tear the paper!

3 The paper will form into gentle curls. If you want tighter curling, the strips can be rolled around the pencil.

Cutting

Paper may be cut in a variety of ways to make interesting designs. Simple cut-outs are especially good for embellishing greetings cards and decorations.

1 Fold a sheet of paper in half. Make horizontal cuts every 3–4 cm (1¼–1½ in) down the fold. Open the paper. Push every second fold backwards to make a step effect.

2 Fold a sheet of paper in half. Make slanting cuts every 2–3 cm (¾–1¼ in) down the fold. Open the paper. Gently pull down each cut between finger and thumb to make small 'tongues'.

3 Fold a piece of paper in half. Cut half a heart shape at equal intervals down the fold. Open the paper to reveal complete hearts down the length of the paper.

Papier-mâché

Papier-mâché is made by shredding paper, usually old newspapers, and combining it with glue. The paper can be used in a number of ways to make a huge variety of objects both useful and just for decoration.

1 For most projects, paper should be torn into fairly short strips approximately 2 cm (¾ in) wide.

2 Mix non-toxic PVA (white) glue with water to the consistency of single (light) cream.

3 Papier-mâché can be pressed into lightly greased moulds or wrapped around cardboard armatures like this.

4 To cover smaller shapes, use small, thin pieces of newspaper.

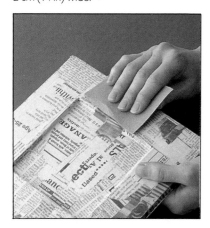

5 Your papier-mâché object may have a slightly rough surface when it has dried out. To make it uniformly smooth, lightly rub the papier-mâché with fine sandpaper.

6 Prime your papier-mâché with two coats of non-toxic white paint to conceal the newsprint surface before decorating.

Stencilling

Stencilling is a way of applying decoration to a surface using special card (cardboard), clear film or metal stencils. A shape is drawn onto the card, cut out, and then paint is applied over the cut-out portion of the stencil with a sponge or brush. It is possible to buy ready-cut stencils or you can make your own. Ask an adult to cut out your stencil motif for you – craft knives are *very* sharp, and are difficult to control.

1 Cut a piece of stencil card (cardboard) and draw your design.

2 Ask an adult to cut out the image from the stencil card.

3 Mix paint in a palette or on an old saucer. Add a little water to make a slightly sticky consistency.

4 Cut a piece of household sponge into small squares.

5 Place the stencil card on a piece of heavy paper or thin card (posterboard). Dip the sponge in paint and gently dab it over the cut-out motif.

6 Remove the stencil card carefully, one corner at a time, to avoid smudging the paint.

Sponging

This is a way of applying paint to a surface using sponges to give a patchy, holey effect. If you use a variety of sponges with different-sized holes you can make very interesting and exciting patterns. Similarly, different colours can be sponged on top of each other if the paint is dry before adding the next colour.

Printing with foam rubber stamps

Simple stamps can be cut from sheets of thin foam rubber and stuck onto cardboard bases. The stamps can be used several times if the excess paint is used up on scrap paper between colours.

1 Cut a piece of household sponge into small squares.

1 To make the stamps, cut several rectangles of heavy cardboard measuring 5 × 6 cm (2 × 2¼ in). Cut an equal number of smaller rectangles measuring 1.5 × 6 cm (⅝ × 2¼ in) to form the handles. Stick the handles to the tops of the bases with strong glue.

2 Dip a piece of sponge into slightly sticky paint and press it lightly onto paper of a contrasting colour.

3 When the paint has dried, sponge a second colour on top to make a bright pattern. When dry the paper may be used to wrap a parcel, as a greetings card or for many other projects in this book.

2 Draw the stamp motif onto foam rubber. Cut it out with scissors and glue it to the cardboard base. Allow to dry thoroughly.

3 Mix a little paint with water to a stiff consistency. Gently dip the stamp in the paint and then press it onto medium-weight paper or thin card (posterboard).

Tracing

Some of the projects in this book include templates that you can copy when you are creating your paper projects. Tracing is the fastest and simplest way to transfer a template to another sheet of paper.

1 Lay a sheet of tracing paper over the template. Carefully trace over the image with a soft pencil to make a dark line.

2 Turn the tracing over. Scribble over the lines with a soft pencil.

3 Place the tracing the right way up on appropriate paper. Draw over the original lines. When the tracing is removed, the image will have been transferred.

Scaling-up

If you want to make a project larger than the template you can scale it up using graph paper. Use a scale of, say, one square on the template to two squares on the graph paper. You may use a different scale depending on the size you want.

1 If you wish to copy a template that is not printed on a grid, trace it and transfer it to graph paper. If the template you have chosen does appear on a grid, as in this book, proceed directly to step 2.

2 Using an appropriate scale, enlarge the template onto a second sheet of graph paper, copying the shape from each smaller square to the larger square.

3 Cut out the new template and transfer it to card (posterboard) or paper.

TEMPLATES

*S*ome of the projects in this book need templates. You can either trace the templates directly from the book, or scale up to the size required following the instructions given earlier.

papier-mâché brooches

papier-mâché Christmas decorations

spinner

letter file and stationery folder

Christmas wreath

dressing-up doll

Christmas wreath

eye mask

finger puppets

*papier-mâché
mirror frame*

foil-covered frame

crocodile

papier-mâché
earrings

Paper Decorations

Bird Mosaic Tray

This tray will make the simplest meal look exciting! Mosaic has been used as a decorative device for centuries, and especially fine examples were made by the Romans to decorate the floors of their villas. The look of mosaic has been imitated here by the use of irregular squares cut from scraps of coloured paper. The tray is sealed with several coats of varnish so it can be wiped clean with a damp cloth after use.

YOU WILL NEED
wooden tray
fine sandpaper
diluted non-toxic PVA (white) glue
paintbrushes
non-toxic white paint
non-toxic bright paint
scissors
thin paper in a variety of colours
pencil
non-toxic clear gloss varnish
  (optional)

paint

sandpaper

scissors

paintbrushes

paper glue

pencil

paper

1 Rub down the surface of the wooden tray with fine sandpaper. Seal the tray with a coat of diluted PVA (white) glue.

2 Prime the tray with a coat of white paint and allow to dry.

3 Paint the tray with two coats of bright paint and allow to dry thoroughly.

4 Cut mosaic squares from sheets of brightly coloured thin paper. Dip each in diluted PVA glue and use a paintbrush to stick in place around the tray.

5 Draw and cut a bird shape from paper and stick it in place in the centre of the tray. Add details cut from contrasting papers and allow the tray to dry overnight.

6 Seal the tray with several coats of diluted PVA glue or clear gloss varnish.

Painted Postcards

Be original and make your own cards. This ingenious method of applying and scratching off paint gives very professional looking results, and the cards could be used for place names and invitations to special events as well as birthdays and Christmas.

YOU WILL NEED
heavy coloured paper
ruler
pencil
scissors
gold paper
paintbrush
non-toxic paint in a variety of colours
non-toxic paper glue

paintbrush

gold paper

paint

ruler

pencil

scissors

paper

paper glue

1 Measure and cut out rectangles of coloured paper measuring 10 × 12 cm (4 × 4¾ in).

2 Cut smaller rectangles of gold paper.

3 Apply a coat of paint to the gold paper, and while it is still wet draw a simple design in the paint with a soft pencil. Allow the paint to dry thoroughly.

4 Cut around the scratched images leaving a small border. Stick each one to a rectangle of coloured paper with paper glue and allow to dry.

Printed Wrapping Paper

If you don't like the gift wrap you see in stationery shops, print your own using stamps cut from foam rubber. It is very satisfying to be congratulated on wrapping paper *and* gift!

YOU WILL NEED
heavy corrugated cardboard
pencil
ruler
scissors
non-toxic strong glue
foam rubber approximately 6 mm
 (¼ in) thick
non-toxic paint in a variety of colours
thin coloured paper

paint

strong glue

foam rubber

scissors

corrugated cardboard

paper

1 To make the stamps, cut several rectangles of heavy cardboard measuring 5 × 6 cm (2 × 2¼ in). Cut an equal number of smaller rectangles measuring 6 × 1.5 cm (2¼ × ⅝ in) to form the handles. Stick the handles to the top of the bases and leave to dry.

2 Draw the image for each stamp onto the piece of foam rubber. Carefully cut around each shape with scissors ensuring that the edges are smooth.

3 Stick the shapes to the base of each stamp and allow to dry thoroughly.

4 Spread a thin layer of paint onto a saucer to act as an ink pad. Press each stamp into the paint, varying the colours as desired, and print the wrapping paper

Decoupage Frame

Decoupage is a form of decoration using pictures cut from magazines, newspapers, even wallpaper. The pictures are then stuck onto mirror frames, screens and all sorts of objects to make a new and interesting design. Black and white pictures can be hand-tinted with paint that matches or contrasts with the object you are decorating. You can dip the pictures in cold tea to give the paper a pleasing 'aged' effect similar to old photos, or you can colour them with paints.

YOU WILL NEED
painted picture frame
sandpaper
assorted black and white pictures
scissors
non-toxic paint that matches the
    colour of the frame
undiluted non-toxic PVA (white) glue
paintbrush
non-toxic clear gloss varnish

sandpaper

frame

pictures

paintbrush

paint

1 Remove the glass and backing from the picture frame. Lightly rub down the paint with sandpaper to give a patchy, antiqued effect.

2 Carefully trim the pictures, leaving a slight border around the edges.

3 Make a thin solution of paint and dip each cut-out briefly into it until the paper is stained. Leave the cuttings flat to dry.

4 Arrange the dried cut-outs around the frame. When you are pleased with the composition, stick them in place with PVA (white) glue.

5 Seal the frame with three or four coats of gloss varnish. Leave to dry.

6 Fit your picture inside and replace the glass and backing.

Woven Paper Cards

Paper weaving is a fun way to achieve exciting effects from a very simple process. Pick your papers with care so that the colours complement each other, or contrast in interesting ways. You can use the weaving as a design on its own, or mount it behind shaped frames to make unusual greetings cards.

YOU WILL NEED
medium-weight card (posterboard) in
   a variety of colours
ruler
pencil
scissors
heavy paper in a variety of colours
non-toxic paper glue

scissors

pencil

ruler

paper

paper glue

card
(posterboard)

1 Draw a rectangle measuring 16 × 24 cm (6¼ × 9½ in) on medium-weight green card (posterboard) and cut it out. Draw a line down the centre of the rectangle and, with adult help, gently score along it with scissors to form a fold.

2 Mark a 9 cm (3½ in) square on the front of the card and cut it out to form a window.

3 Cut a piece of red card measuring 10 × 10 cm (4 × 4 in). Make vertical cuts every 1 cm (⅜ in) down the card, from just below the top edge almost to the bottom, but do not cut all the way through.

4 Cut several strips of orange paper approximately 1 cm (⅜ in) wide.

5 Weave the orange strips through the red to make a checked pattern. Trim and attach the orange strips at each side of the card with paper glue.

6 Stick the woven square to the inside front of the card so that it shows through the window.

Spinner

An alternative to the traditional wooden die is this spinning hexagonal version. You could make it with more sides and higher numbers to make board games more exciting. You will need to use simple geometry if you want to make an eight or ten-sided shape.

YOU WILL NEED
tracing paper
pencil
medium-weight card (posterboard)
scissors
thin red paper
thin blue paper
non-toxic paper glue
scraps of coloured paper
thin coloured card (posterboard)

scissors

pencil

paper glue

card
(posterboard)

tracing paper

paper

1 Trace the spinner from the template and transfer it to the medium-weight card (posterboard).

2 Cut out the spinner shape and draw around it on red and blue paper. Cut out the shapes you have drawn and stick them to the front and back of the card.

3 Cut thin strips of orange paper and stick them to the red side of the spinner in a star formation to give six sections. Draw the numbers 1 to 6 on scraps of coloured paper, cut them out and stick them in sequence around the spinner.

4 Draw and cut a spinning stick from thin coloured card. With adult help, make a small slit in the centre of the spinner and insert the stick through the slit.

Calendar

Picture postcards are an ideal source of attractive images to decorate a calendar. Remember to choose your picture with care and use one that you particularly like – perhaps a favourite holiday destination – because you'll be looking at it for a whole year!

YOU WILL NEED
medium-weight card (posterboard)
ruler
pencil
scissors
green and orange paper
non-toxic paper glue
picture
small calendar
hole punch
thin cord

scissors

hole punch

calendar

pencil

paper glue

cord

card (posterboard)

ruler

paper

1 Measure and cut out a rectangle 15 × 24 cm (6 × 9½ in) from the card (posterboard).

2 Cut a piece of green paper the same size and stick it on the card.

3 Cut two strips of orange paper 3 × 15 cm (1¼ × 6 in). Cut triangles from one edge of each strip of paper to make a zig-zag pattern. Stick these at the top and bottom of the board.

4 Cut your chosen picture to size and stick it in place on the card. Stick the calendar below it. Punch holes in the top of the card and tie cord through the holes to form a hanger.

Paper Chains

One of the quickest and most effective ways to transform a room for Christmas is to make garlands of bright paper chains. Crêpe, shiny or novelty papers all make very fine decorations. As an alternative, why not use different-coloured newspapers for unusual recycled paper chains?

YOU WILL NEED
thin paper in a variety of colours
ruler
pencil
scissors
non-toxic paper glue
stapler

pencil

scissors

ruler

paper glue

stapler

paper

1 Cut strips of coloured paper measuring 2.5 × 16 cm (1 × 6¼ in).

2 Cut narrow strips of contrasting paper 16 cm (6¼ in) long.

3 Using paper glue, stick the contrasts to the paper strips. Allow them to dry.

4 Bend a decorated strip into a circle and, with adult help, staple the ends together. Interlock a second strip of paper through the first, and again staple the ends. Continue to form a chain.

Christmas Decorations

These decorations, based on snowflake formations, will really brighten your tree with their vivid colours, and they're so much cheaper than glass baubles! Make an especially large and colourful design for the top of the tree.

YOU WILL NEED
medium-weight paper in a variety of colours
ruler
pencil
scissors
paper ribbon
stapler
non-toxic paper glue

pencil

scissors

ruler

stapler

paper ribbon

paper glue

paper

1 Cut four strips of paper each measuring 15 cm (6 in) long and approximately 1 cm (⅜ in) wide. Cut a length of paper ribbon to make a hanger.

2 Place the strips of paper in a star formation. Make a loop with the paper ribbon and place it in the centre of the star. With adult help, staple the strips and ribbon together.

3 Carefully snip each strip of paper up the middle to within 1 cm (⅜ in) of the centre of the decoration. Roll the resulting thin strips of paper around a pencil to curl them.

4 Cut small circles of contrasting paper and stick them at the centre of the decoration to hide the staple.

Christmas Wreath

Celebrate the festive season with this Christmas wreath. The leaves are lightly scored so that they have a three-dimensional effect. Use gold paper to impart an extra sparkle to the musical angel.

YOU WILL NEED
heavy red paper
ruler
pencil
scissors
tracing paper
green, white, gold and pink paper
small stapler
non-toxic paper glue
paper ribbon
thin cord

scissors

paper glue

gold paper

stapler

paper ribbon

pencil

tracing paper

paper

cord

1 Draw a circle measuring 24 cm (9½ in) in diameter on a square of heavy red paper. Cut it out.

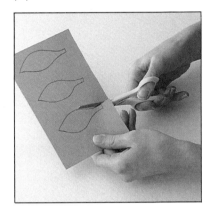

2 Trace the leaf shape from the template and transfer it to the green paper. Cut out approximately 30 leaves.

3 To make the leaves appear three-dimensional, ask an adult to help you score the centre of each one with a pair of scissors and curve the paper. Score half the leaves on the front and half on the back, so that they curve around the right- and left-hand sides of the wreath.

4 With adult help, staple the leaves around both sides of the wreath, overlapping them slightly.

5 Trace the angel pieces from the template and transfer them to white, gold and pink paper. Cut out each of the pieces, and stick them in place on the front of the wreath.

6 Open out a length of paper ribbon and tie it to form a bow. Stick it in position at the bottom of the wreath. Stick a loop of cord to the back to form a hanger.

Papier-mâché Christmas Decorations

These Christmas decorations are fun to make and will look special on your Christmas tree. They make great gifts, too. They could simply be painted as an alternative to sponging if you prefer a smooth finish.

YOU WILL NEED
tracing paper or graph paper
heavy corrugated cardboard
pencil
scissors
newspaper
diluted non-toxic PVA (white) glue
paintbrushes
non-toxic white paint
non-toxic dark red and gold paints
small sponge
darning needle
non-toxic strong glue
eye pins
gold cord

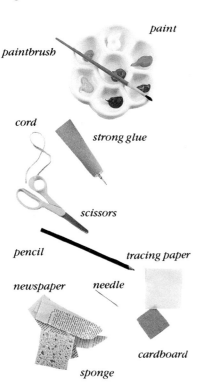

paint

paintbrush

cord

strong glue

scissors

pencil

tracing paper

newspaper

needle

cardboard

sponge

1 Trace or scale up the decorations from the template at the beginning of the book and transfer to the cardboard. Cut them out.

2 Cover each cardboard shape with three layers of papier-mâché. Let them dry overnight.

3 Prime the decorations with two coats of white paint.

4 Paint the decorations dark red. Add a second coat of paint if necessary.

5 Dab gold paint over each decoration with a sponge to give a mottled pattern.

6 With adult help, make a hole in the top of each decoration with a darning needle. Dab a little strong glue over the hole and push in an eye pin. When the glue has dried, tie a length of gold cord through the eye pin.

Cork Place Mats

Make meal times fun with these bright place mats.
They are decorated with colourful turtle motifs cut
from bright paper – but you can make a set with
additional animal designs. The mats can't be washed,
but can be wiped clean with a damp cloth after use.

YOU WILL NEED
cork place mats
non-toxic clear gloss varnish
paintbrush
non-toxic bright paint
pencil
thin paper in a variety of colours
scissors
non-toxic PVA (white) glue

paint

place mat

paintbrush

scissors

pencil

paper

1 Seal the cork mats with a coat of clear gloss varnish and allow them to dry for a couple of hours.

2 Prime the mats with two coats of brightly coloured paint and allow them to dry overnight.

3 Draw each piece of the turtle motif on coloured paper and cut out.

4 Apply a coat of PVA (white) glue to the back of each piece of paper and stick it in position on the mat. Brush over the paper with PVA glue. When the mat is dry, seal it with several coats of varnish.

Rubber-stamped Stationery

If you're looking for unusual stationery, why not cut stamps from small erasers to decorate writing paper and envelopes? You could press them onto different-coloured ink pads or into bright paint to make your own personal stationery. You must ask an adult to cut the eraser for you – craft knives are *very* sharp.

YOU WILL NEED
pencil
rubber erasers
craft knife
non-toxic ink pad
writing paper

ink pad

pencil

erasers

writing paper

1 Draw your design onto the face of the eraser.

2 Ask an adult to trim carefully around the design with a craft knife to leave a raised image.

3 Gently press the eraser onto the ink pad. Test it first on a scrap of paper to make sure that enough ink has been absorbed to make a dark image.

4 Press the eraser firmly onto the writing paper. Remove it carefully to avoid smudging the ink.

Stencilled Frieze

Print your own frieze using card (cardboard) stencils.
Paint is applied through the stencils with small
sponges to give a patchy, mottled effect. Re-tell your
favourite tale on a frieze – this one depicts the animals
fleeing to Noah's Ark to escape the flood waters. You
must ask an adult to cut out the stencils for you – craft
knives are *very* sharp.

YOU WILL NEED
thin coloured card (posterboard)
ruler
pencil
scissors
stencil card (cardboard)
craft knife
non-toxic paint in a variety of colours
palette or old china saucer
squares of household sponge
non-toxic paper glue (optional)

paint

*stencil card
(cardboard)*

pencil

scissors

ruler

paper glue

sponge

*card
(posterboard)*

saucer

1 Measure and cut out a length of thin card (posterboard) 25 × 90 cm (10 × 36 in) or two pieces 25 × 46 cm (10 × 18 in).

2 Draw various animal shapes, an ark, clouds and water on rectangles of waxed stencil card (cardboard).

3 Ask an adult to cut out each stencil for you using a craft knife.

4 Place the stencils in position on the thin card. Squeeze a small amount of paint onto your palette or old saucer. Using a square of sponge, gently dab paint over the area exposed by the first stencil. Carefully lift the stencil from the card.

5 Continue blocking each stencil using appropriately coloured paint. Add a row of clouds at the top of the frieze, and water beneath the animals.

6 Allow the frieze to dry thoroughly, and glue it together if more than one sheet of card has been used.

PAPER PROJECTS

Stained-glass Horse

Here's a simple way to imitate beautiful stained-glass windows. These decorations are most effective when hung at a window as the light shines through the tissue paper, bringing it to life. However, they would look great on a Christmas tree as well.

YOU WILL NEED
black cartridge (construction) paper
white pencil
scissors
tissue paper in a variety of colours
non-toxic paper glue
thin ribbon or cord

tissue paper

scissors

paper glue   *ribbon*

white pencil

cartridge (construction) paper

1 Draw a horse shape onto black paper with a white pencil. Add star decorations. Cut out the horse shape.

2 Draw around the shape on a second piece of black paper and cut this out.

3 Using a pair of scissors, carefully cut out the star shapes and features from the first horse. Place this horse on top of the second horse shape and transfer the cut-out motifs with a white pencil. Cut out the decorations from the second horse.

4 Cut small pieces of tissue paper in various colours and stick them to the back of one horse shape over the cut-outs.

5 When all the cut-outs are covered, stick a small loop of ribbon or cord to the top back of the horse.

6 Stick the second horse shape to the back of the first. Carefully trim the edges of the horse if necessary.

Monster Feet

Disguise your hands with these colourful monster feet! They're great fun for parties and, as they cover only the backs of your hands, you will still be able to eat and drink a monstrous amount!

YOU WILL NEED
heavy coloured paper
pencil
scissors
thin paper in contrasting colours
non-toxic paper glue
paper clips (optional)

paper glue

pencil

scissors

paper

I Draw a five-toed monster foot on the heavy paper. Cut it out and use it as a template to make a second foot. Remember to cut an extension of paper from each ankle to form a fastening band.

2 Place the monster feet on thin coloured paper. Draw around the tip of each toe and cut out the shapes to make toenails. Stick each toenail to its corresponding toe.

3 Cut out polka dots from a third coloured paper. Stick these in position on the fronts of the feet.

4 Wrap the fastening bands around your wrists and ask a friend to mark the point where they overlap. Trim if necessary and cut notches to form a fastening, or attach with paper clips.

Crocodile

You can make a whole menagerie of animals by cutting and folding thin card. Split paper fasteners are good for joining limbs to bodies, for they allow a certain amount of movement in the animals.

YOU WILL NEED
tracing paper or graph paper
pencil
thin blue card (posterboard)
scissors
scraps of white and contrasting paper
non-toxic paper glue
black pen
split paper fasteners
sticky tape

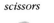

paper glue

pen   *pencil*

scissors

paper   *tracing paper*

card (posterboard)

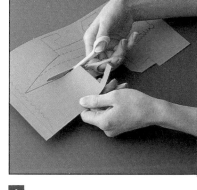

1 Trace or scale up the crocodile from the template. Transfer it to the thin blue card (posterboard). Cut out the body and jaw piece. Cut eye lines.

2 With adult help, score the crocodile's body along the dotted lines. Gently bend the crocodile along the scorings to make it three-dimensional.

3 Cut diamonds of contrasting paper and stick them along the crocodile's back. Stick white paper over its eyes, and draw a dot on both with a black pen to represent pupils.

4 With adult help, make a small slit on either side of the crocodile's head and the jaw piece as indicated. Push a split paper fastener through the slits to fix the jaw to the head. Open the shanks of the pin on the inside of the crocodile and fix in position with tape.

Dressing-up Doll

Shiver me timbers! Here's a brawny brigand for you to dress! Why not make a parrot to sit on his shoulder and keep him company on the high seas?

YOU WILL NEED
tracing paper or graph paper
pencil
thin white card (posterboard)
cartridge (construction) paper
scissors
paintbrushes
non-toxic paint in a variety of colours

paint

paintbrush

pencil

scissors

card (posterboard)

tracing paper

cartridge (construction) paper

1 Trace or scale up the pirate and his clothes from the template at the beginning of the book.

2 Transfer the pirate to thin card (posterboard), and the clothes to cartridge (construction) paper. Carefully cut them out.

3 Fill in the pirate's features with paint. Paint his underclothes in bright colours and decorate the pirate's clothes.

4 With adult help, lightly score and fold the base of the pirate so that he stands up.

5 Bend the tabs of the clothes over. Place them on the pirate and squeeze the tabs closed so that they fit snugly over the paper figure.

Space Mobile

Join the space race with this lunar mobile! Careful attachment of the suspension threads will ensure that each piece hangs square. You will have to decorate each piece on both sides as the mobile will rotate gently in the breeze.

YOU WILL NEED
stiff paper in a variety of colours
pencil
scissors
non-toxic paper glue
darning needle
thin nylon thread

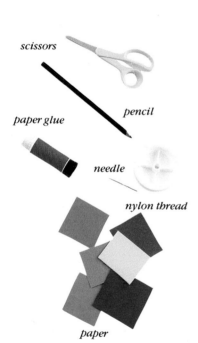

scissors

paper glue   *pencil*

needle

nylon thread

paper

1 Draw rocket, astronaut and moon shapes on appropriately coloured stiff paper. Cut them out.

2 Cut decorative additions from scraps of coloured paper and stick them on both sides of the shapes.

3 Hold each shape between finger and thumb to test its centre of gravity so that it will hang straight. With adult help, make a hole at this point with a darning needle.

4 Cut lengths of nylon thread and tie one end through the hole at the top of each shape.

5 Assemble the mobile. The smaller rocket is the first piece in the structure. With adult help, make a hole in the bottom centre of this piece and hang the larger rocket from it. Make three holes along the bottom of the larger rocket to suspend the astronauts and moon.

6 Tie the nylon thread that is attached to the smaller rocket into a loop and use this to suspend the mobile.

Monocle Disguise

Wear this monocle when you want to remain incognito! It's always good fun to make disguises – let your imagination run wild and make several for special occasions or festivities.

YOU WILL NEED
medium-weight paper in a variety of
    colours
pencil
scissors
non-toxic paper glue
thin cord
darning needle
 thin elastic cord

thin elastic cord

scissors

needle

cord

pencil

paper
glue

paper

1 Draw nose, moustache, eyebrow and monocle pieces on coloured paper and cut them out.

2 With adult help, carefully score a central line down the nose to make a fold. Score along the centres of the moustache pieces following the curve and fold them into shape.

3 Assemble the eye and monocle and stick it in place on the nose. Stick the remaining pieces – eyebrows, moustache and monocle cord – in place.

4 With adult help, make two holes in the side of each eyebrow with a darning needle. Push the ends of a length of thin elastic through the holes and knot them, so that the elastic fits your head.

Sun and Moon Masks

Groups of masks on the same theme look very
effective when seen together. Make some to illustrate
well-known partnerships such as cat and mouse, stars
and stripes, or the three wise monkeys.

YOU WILL NEED
heavy blue and yellow paper
pencil
scissors
scraps of thin orange paper
non-toxic paper glue
darning needle
thin elastic cord

pencil   *scissors*

needle

thin elastic cord

paper glue

paper

1 Draw a moon shape on the blue
paper. Remember to make it large
enough to cover half your face. Cut out
the shape.

2 Cut a star shape from thin orange
paper and stick it to the front of the
moon shape with paper glue.

3 With adult help, make holes in each
side of the mask with a darning needle.
Push the ends of a length of thin elastic
or ribbon through the holes and knot
them so the elastic fits your head.

4 Cut a sun shape from heavy yellow
paper. Cut out eye holes and stick small
pieces of orange paper to the front of the
sun as rays. With adult help, make holes in
the sides of the mask and thread through
a length of elastic or ribbon. Tie a knot at
each end to keep it in place.

Eye Masks

Even if you're not going to a masked ball, you'll have fun making and wearing these disguises! They're especially good if you're in a play or pantomime – you'll be surprised how difficult your friends find it to recognize you!

YOU WILL NEED
tracing paper or graph paper
pencil
thin card (posterboard) in a variety of colours
scissors
paper in a variety of colours
non-toxic paper glue
thin wooden sticks
paintbrush
non-toxic paint
non-toxic strong glue
wax crayons
gold paper

wooden stick
gold paper
strong glue
scissors
crayons
pencil
paper glue
paper
tracing paper
paint

1 Trace or scale up the fiery mask shape from the template at the beginning of the book and transfer to orange card (posterboard). Cut it out.

2 Place the card on purple paper. Extend the sides and top of the eye mask with small spikes. Cut out this shape.

3 Using paper glue stick the orange shape in place on top of the purple one. Carefully trim the lower edge of the mask if necessary.

4 Paint the wooden stick a bright colour. You may have to use two coats of paint.

5 Attach the wooden stick to the side of the mask with strong glue. Stick it the right of the mask if you are right-handed and vice-versa if you are left-handed.

6 To make the leopard mask, use yellow card and apply the spots with wax crayon. The king has a crown made of gold paper, and his eyebrows are applied with wax crayon.

Cowboy Face Mask

Ride the range in this cowboy mask! Wear a bright scarf around your neck for added authenticity and you'll be the envy of every cowpoke in town!

YOU WILL NEED
heavy light blue, dark blue and orange paper
pencil
scissors ruler
non-toxic paper glue
sticky tape
stapler

scissors

stapler

sticky tape

pencil

paper glue

paper

1 Draw a hat on the light blue paper. Draw a thin band approximately 5 × 60 cm (2 × 24 in) on the same paper. Cut them out.

2 Draw a steer's head on the orange paper and cut it out. Stick it to the front of the hat with paper glue.

3 Draw and cut out the eye mask from the dark blue paper. Stick it to the back of the hat with sticky tape.

4 Stick the hat band to the back of the hat with paper glue. Make sure that it is not visible from the front. To give additional strength, hold the band in place with a strip of sticky tape. Hold the hat band around the head and ask a friend to mark where the two ends overlap. Remove the hat and with adult help, staple or glue the ends neatly together.

Stencilled Snap Cards

A game of snap is always good fun – why not make your own set of cards like this cheerful version? The cards are stencilled with different colours and are bright and simple. Each stencil can be used several times if allowed to dry thoroughly between colours. You must ask an adult to cut out the stencils for you – craft knives are *very* sharp.

YOU WILL NEED
stencil card (cardboard)
ruler
pencil
scissors
craft knife
heavy paper in four different colours
small squares of household sponge
non-toxic paint in four different
   colours
non-toxic paper glue
medium-weight coloured card
   (posterboard)

ruler
stencil card
(cardboard)
paint
scissors
sponge
paper
glue
pencil
card
(posterboard)
paper

1 Cut four pieces of stencil card (cardboard) measuring approximately 6 × 9 cm (2¼ × 3½ in).

2 Draw four different symbols on the stencil card. Ask an adult to cut out the shapes for you with a craft knife.

3 Cut rectangles of coloured paper measuring 6.5 × 8.5 cm (2½ × 3¼ in). Place the first stencil on one of the rectangles. With a sponge square, dab paint over the stencil until the cut-out space is covered. Carefully remove the stencil, taking care not to smudge the paint. Repeat with all the stencils until you have made enough cards.

4 Stick each stencilled rectangle onto a slightly larger piece of medium-weight card (posterboard). Allow the glue to dry thoroughly before you play snap.

PLAYING SNAP

To play, deal out all the cards to each player. In turn, discard one card onto a central pile. If two cards of the same pair are played in sequence, the first player to notice must shout 'snap' and grab the pair. The player with the most pairs at the end of the game wins. It sounds simple, but try playing very quickly!

Crowns

You'll need a regal bearing to wear these colourful crowns. Their unusual shape comes from the simple folding and looping of medium-weight paper to very stylish effect.

YOU WILL NEED
medium-weight paper in a variety of
  colours
ruler
pencil
scissors
stapler
sticky tape
non-toxic paper glue

pencil

ruler

scissors

stapler

paper glue

paper

1 Measure and cut out a large rectangle 19 × 60 cm (7½ × 24 in) from medium-weight paper.

2 Mark a point 7 cm (2¾ in) from the bottom of the rectangle. Draw a central line from side to side. Draw a vertical line from the top of the rectangle to this line every 2 cm (¾ in).

3 Carefully cut down these lines stopping at the lower horizontal line. Cut off the final strip of paper to make a fastening tab.

4 Carefully bring down each strip of paper to form a loop and with adult help, staple the loops to the remaining strip of paper. Continue all the way around the crown. Bend both ends round to meet and staple and tape the crown at the join.

5 Cut a strip of paper 6 × 58 cm (2¼ × 23 in) from paper of a contrasting colour. Draw a central line dividing the strip in half. Make small notches along one edge of the strip up to the central line. Stick this strip around the base of the crown, folding the notched edge to the inside of the crown, to form a band.

6 Cut ovals of bright paper to represent jewels and stick them around the crown.

Finger Puppets

Finger puppets are quick and easy to make, and are especially good for entertaining very young children at bed time. If you make familiar characters from books, you can perform short plays to accompany fairy stories and folk tales.

YOU WILL NEED
tracing paper
pencil
medium-weight coloured paper in a
   variety of colours
scissors
non-toxic paper glue

pencil

paper glue

tracing
paper

scissors

paper

1 Trace the pig and wolf shapes from the templates. Transfer the wolf to orange paper and the pig three times to pink. Cut out each animal.

2 Cut eyes and noses for each animal from small scraps of coloured paper and stick them in place with paper glue.

3 Cut a small strip of paper approximately 2 cm (¾ in) wide and long enough to fit around your fingers for each puppet. Stick each animal in the centre of a strip.

4 Stick the ends of each finger band together. Allow the puppets to dry thoroughly before playing with them.

Magnetic Fish Game

This is a version of an old and much-loved game that has been played by generations of children. To make the game more competitive, you could write a score on the back of each fish. The player with the highest score wins.

YOU WILL NEED
scraps of heavy coloured paper
pencil
scissors
wax crayons
paper clips
thin wooden sticks
thin coloured cord
small horseshoe magnet

scissors

pencil

cord

magnet

paper clips

wooden stick

paper

crayons

1 Draw fish shapes onto the scraps of paper and cut them out.

2 Decorate the fish using wax crayons.

3 Attach a paper clip to the nose of each fish so that it can be picked up by the fishing line.

4 To make the fishing rod, tie a length of cord to the wooden dowel and tie a small magnet to the end of the line.

Horse Tableau

This desert scene could be used as a centrepiece for a party spread. You could make smaller versions for each individual place setting for exciting and unusual table decorations.

YOU WILL NEED
yellow card (posterboard)
pencil
ruler
scissors
heavy paper in a variety of colours
sticky tape
non-toxic paper glue

ruler

scissors

pencil

card (posterboard)

paper

1 Draw a rectangle measuring 15 × 20 cm (6 × 8 in) on yellow card (posterboard). Cut it out.

2 Draw a horse shape on brown paper. Draw a cactus and a strip of grass on green paper. Draw another cactus on red paper. Cut out all these shapes. Add the horse's features with scraps of coloured paper.

3 Cut small circles of coloured paper and snip around the edges to make 'flowers'.

4 Mark where the horse and cacti will stand on the yellow card. With adult help, make thin slits in the card at these points with a pair of scissors.

5 The horse, cacti and strip of grass should be scored, with adult help, to make tabs approximately 1 cm (⅜ in) wide. Fold over each tab, and insert the horse and cacti in appropriate slits in the yellow card. Stick them in position.

6 Stick the flowers on the yellow card around the horse and cacti and stick the strip of grass along the front of the card.

Noughts and Crosses (Tic-Tac-Toe)

This old favourite has been brought up to date with bright jazzy colours. You could make this a portable game for journeys and holidays – use some scraps of card to form a small carrying case for board and cards.

YOU WILL NEED
medium-weight card (posterboard)
ruler
pencil
scissors
thick pink, yellow, green and blue paper
non-toxic paper glue

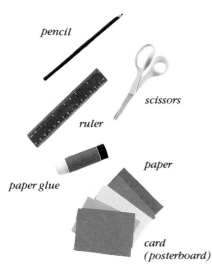

pencil

scissors

ruler

paper

paper glue

card (posterboard)

1 Mark out a square measuring 20 × 20 cm (8 × 8 in) on medium-weight card (posterboard). Cut out the square.

2 Place the cardboard square on the pink paper and draw around it. Cut out the paper square and stick it to the card.

3 Cut a smaller square of card measuring 15 × 15 cm (6 × 6 in). Cut a piece of yellow paper the same size.

4 Stick the yellow paper to the card and cut the card into nine squares each measuring 5 × 5 cm (2 × 2 in).

5 Cut four strips of green paper 15 × 1 cm (6 × ⅜ in). Stick them to the pink board to form nine equal squares.

6 Draw noughts and crosses (X's and O's) on the pink and blue paper. Cut them out and stick them to the yellow squares to complete the cards.

Garden Hat

You'll be the star of the garden party in this lovely, leafy hat. Add butterflies for extra excitement!

YOU WILL NEED
thin green card (posterboard)
ruler
pencil
scissors
heavy paper in a variety of colours
non-toxic paper glue

pencil

ruler

scissors

paper glue

card (poster-board)

paper

1 Draw a rectangle measuring 22 × 60 cm (8¾ × 24 in) on green card (posterboard). Using the photograph as a guide, mark out the hat on the card. The triangles along the front of the hat should be drawn to varying lengths as they form the stalks of the flowers.

2 Cut out the hat shape, remembering to cut the stalks to different lengths.

3 To make the flowers, cut circles of heavy paper in various bright colours. Snip small pieces of paper from around the edges of each circle to make petal shapes. Decorate each flower with details cut from contrasting paper, and stick in place with paper glue.

4 Cut butterflies from coloured paper and add their markings with scraps of bright paper.

5 Stick the flowers and butterflies around the hat.

6 Hold the hat around your head and ask a friend to mark where the two ends of the hat band meet. Cut a notch in each end of the band to form a fastening.

Jigsaw

Jigsaws are a great source of enjoyment for many people. This one is cut into simple wavy pieces that slot neatly together. You could make small puzzles and give them as combined greetings cards and presents.

YOU WILL NEED
heavy card (posterboard)
ruler
pencil
scissors
stiff paper in a variety of colours
non-toxic paper glue
hole punch
craft knife (optional)

hole punch

pencil

scissors

paper glue

paper

card (posterboard)

1 Measure and cut out a piece of card (posterboard) 20 × 24 cm (8 × 9½ in).

2 Place the card on a sheet of stiff blue paper and draw around it. Cut out the paper and stick it to the card.

3 Cut a fish shape from yellow paper and tail pieces from orange. Cut scale shapes from red and orange paper. Cut shells from different colours.

4 Stick the scales and other additions to the fish, then stick the fish to the card. Stick the shells to the background.

5 Cut a strip of purple paper to the same width as the card. Trim the edges into a wavy pattern and make a decorative pattern with the hole punch. Stick the water on the card.

6 Draw nine uneven sections on the back of the board. Carefully cut along the lines with a pair of scissors, or ask an adult to cut using a craft knife.

Cat Papercut Picture

The ancient art of papercutting has been practised in Eastern countries for many years. Make your own decorative cuts and mount them on sheets of contrasting paper. Papercuts make very good gifts and names and dates of birth can be incorporated into the design. You must ask an adult to cut around the design for you as craft knives are *very* sharp.

YOU WILL NEED
heavy paper in contrasting colours
pencil
craft knife
scissors
non-toxic paper glue

pencil

paper glue

scissors

paper

1 Draw your chosen design on one sheet of coloured paper.

2 Ask an adult to carefully cut the excess paper from between the pencil lines to form a framework rather like a stained-glass window.

3 Using scissors, cut a wavy decorative edge around the finished papercut.

4 Cut the second piece of coloured paper slightly larger than the picture. Apply glue to the reverse of the papercut and stick it to the contrasting paper.

Rolled Paper Beads

Simple, effective jewellery can be made by rolling strips of jazzy paper around a pencil. The resulting beads can be used to make necklaces or bracelets.

YOU WILL NEED
decorative paper
ruler
pencil
scissors
non-toxic paper glue
thin cord

cord

pencil

paper glue

scissors

decorative paper

ruler

1 For each bead, cut a strip measuring 4 × 30 cm (1½ × 12 in) from a sheet of decorative paper.

2 Draw tapering lines along each strip of paper so that it measures 1 cm (⅜ in) at one end and 4 cm (1½ in) at the other. Cut away the excess paper.

3 Take a pencil. Wrap the wider end of a paper strip around it. Dab a little glue on the end of the strip and carefully roll the paper around the pencil to make a tubular bead. Glue the narrow end of the strip around the bead, allow to dry, and slip it off the pencil.

4 Repeat the process with the remaining strips to form more beads and when you have enough, string them onto a length of brightly-coloured cord.

Paper Flowers

These everlasting blooms are made by folding and cutting squares of coloured paper into a variety of shapes. Experiment with the technique to make some really fabulous flowers!

YOU WILL NEED
thin coloured paper
ruler
pencil
scissors
non-toxic paper glue
non-toxic strong glue
pipe cleaners

pencil

ruler

scissors

paper glue

pipe cleaners

paper

1 Cut squares of coloured paper measuring 10 × 10 cm (4 × 4 in). Fold each one into quarters.

2 Cut a curve into each folded square so that it will form a circle when opened.

3 Cut a variety of petal shapes into the curved shape. Open out each flower.

4 Cut circles and other details from contrasting paper and stick them with paper glue to the middle of each flower.

5 Using strong glue stick a pipe cleaner to the back of each flower to make a stem. You can make stems of different lengths if you prefer.

6 Cut leaf shapes from green paper. Stick these to short lengths of pipe cleaner with strong glue leaving a 3 cm (1¼ in) 'stem' below each leaf. Wrap this short stem around the main stem of the flower to attach the leaves.

Recycled Paper Greetings Cards

Recycled paper has an appealing, pitted surface that can be very decorative. These cards are collaged from a mixture of different-coloured papers torn from a writing block.

YOU WILL NEED
recycled coloured paper
ruler
pencil
scissors
non-toxic paper glue

scissors

ruler

pencil

paper glue

paper

1 Take a sheet of recycled paper and draw a rectangle measuring 13 × 26 cm (5¼ × 10¼ in). Cut out the shape and fold it in half to make a card.

4 Using paper glue, stick the square border on the front of the folded card. Stick the heart motif in the middle. You can create additional motifs by tearing designs from coloured paper and sticking them onto cards.

2 Take a sheet of contrasting paper and tear a heart shape out of it.

3 Cut a square of paper in a third colour measuring 12 × 12 cm (4¾ × 4¾ in). Fold it in half. Carefully tear out the middle to leave a ragged border.

Fold-out Greetings Card

Fold-out cards are very versatile – they could simply be decorative like this one, or serve a practical purpose as well. For example, you could cut the words 'Please Come to my Party' from brightly coloured paper and stick them to the third panel to make an unusual and exciting invitation.

YOU WILL NEED
blue medium-weight card
  (posterboard)
pencil
ruler
scissors
thin paper in a variety of colours
non-toxic paper glue

paper glue

ruler

pencil

scissors

paper

*card
(posterboard)*

1 Draw a rectangle measuring 36 × 20 cm (14 × 8 in) on the card (posterboard). Cut it out.

2 Measure a point every 9 cm (3½ in) along the top and bottom of the card. Draw three vertical lines and, with adult help, lightly score along them to make three folds. The first and third lines should be scored on the front of the card and the second on the back.

3 Draw and cut out the pieces of each character from various coloured papers.

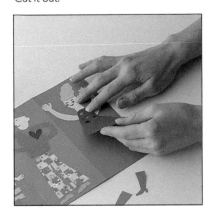

4 Stick the figures in position on each panel of the card using paper glue.

Photograph Album

Keep your favourite photographs in this album and
make more pages as you need them – the cords can be
untied to add new leaves. The album could be used to
make a commemorative record of a special event such
as a wedding or christening, and given as a present.

YOU WILL NEED
medium-weight card (posterboard)
ruler
pencil
scissors
pad of A4 (11¾ × 8½ in) recycled
    paper
hole punch
non-toxic paper glue
thin cord

thin cord

hole punch

paper glue

scissors

*card
(posterboard)*

recycled paper

1 To make the album cover, draw two
rectangles measuring 15 × 22 cm (6 ×
8¾ in) on the card (posterboard). Cut
them out.

2 Take twelve sheets of A4 recycled
paper. Fold each sheet in half and carefully
cut it along the fold to make two sheets of
paper. Make a set of double holes in each
sheet of paper with a hole punch.

3 Following the photograph, notch the
corners of two sheets of recycled paper
to decorate the album cover. Cut out the
paper, and carefully stick each to one of
the rectangles of card.

4 Cut two rectangles of contrasting
paper measuring 21 × 14.5 cm (8½ ×
5¾ in). Stick these to the inside front and
back of the cover.

5 Punch holes in the covers, making
sure that they correspond to those in the
paper. Draw and cut out a simple cover
motif from scraps of paper and stick them
in place on the front of the album.

6 Align covers and paper, and tie a
small piece of cord through the top and
bottom sets of holes. Make the cord
loose enough to allow the pages to be
turned over.

Corrugated Gift Tags

These unusual gift tags, although made from humble cardboard and string, look very stylish. They are especially suitable for gift wrapping items made from natural materials such as wood.

YOU WILL NEED
corrugated cardboard
ruler
pencil
scissors
coloured corrugated card
  (posterboard)
non-toxic paper glue
hole punch
thick coloured twine

hole punch

pencil

scissors

paper glue

*corrugated card
(posterboard)*

twine   *cardboard*

1 Draw label shapes measuring 9 × 6 cm (3½ × 2¼ in) on the corrugated cardboard.

2 Cut rectangles of coloured corrugated card (posterboard) slightly smaller than the gift tags. Stick them on the front of each tag.

3 Cut a zig-zag shape from contrasting coloured corrugated card and stick in place on top of the card rectangles.

4 With adult help, make a hole at the end of each label with a hole punch. Tie a length of twine through each hole.

Paper Gift Tags

What better way to jazz-up a parcel then these cheerful gift tags? Make them in a variety of colours, wrap your parcels in bright, festive papers and parties will go with a swing.

YOU WILL NEED
heavy paper in a variety of colours
ruler
pencil
scissors
thin paper in a variety of colours
non-toxic paper glue
hole punch
coloured cord

hole punch

ruler

scissors

pencil

paper

cord

1 Draw a rectangle measuring 14 × 8.5 cm (5½ × 3¼ in) on heavy coloured paper and cut it out.

2 Draw an animal head on contrasting thin paper. Cut it out.

3 Divide the rectangle of paper in half. Draw a faint line down the centre of the paper and, with adult help, gently score along the line. Fold the card in half.

4 Stick the animal face to the front of the folded card with paper glue. With adult help, make a hole in the top left-hand corner of the back of the card with a hole punch. Tie a loop of cord through the hole.

Fancy Wrapped Parcels

Turn the humblest present into an exciting parcel by making the wrappings interesting and fun. All sorts of characters are appropriate for decorating parcels. Think of the person who will receive the parcel, and of their favourite characters when choosing a design.

YOU WILL NEED
items to wrap
crêpe paper
sticky tape
paper ribbon
pencil
thin paper in a variety of colours
scissors
non-toxic paper glue
non-toxic strong glue

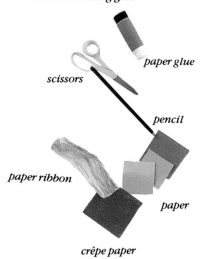

scissors

paper glue

pencil

paper ribbon

paper

crêpe paper

1 Wrap the parcels in crêpe paper.

2 Open out lengths of paper ribbon and secure each parcel.

3 Draw designs onto pieces of thin coloured paper to make the head, arms and legs for each parcel (or head, legs and tail if an animal). Cut out the shapes.

4 Stick the decorative details onto each main body piece with paper glue.

5 Stick the decorations around the corners of each parcel with strong glue.

Bookplates

Some very beautiful bookplate designs have been produced for proud book-owners. Now you can make some for your own library. These are printed using blocks cut from scraps of polystyrene. If the plates are fixed to the books using spray glue, they can be repositioned or removed as you please. You must ask an adult to cut the polystyrene for you – craft knives are *very* sharp.

YOU WILL NEED
small sheet of polystyrene 1.5 cm
 (⅝ in) thick
ruler
pencil
craft knife
non-toxic paint
paintbrush
heavy paper

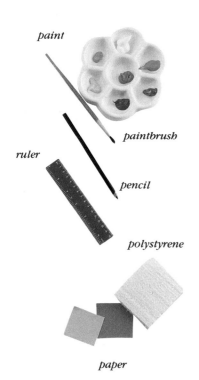

paint

paintbrush

ruler

pencil

polystyrene

paper

1 Draw a rectangle measuring 6 × 9 cm (2¼ × 3½ in) on a sheet of polystyrene. Ask an adult to cut it out for you using a craft knife.

2 Draw a geometric design on one side of the rectangle. Ask an adult to carefully cut around your design with a craft knife to leave a raised pattern.

3 Apply paint to the raised parts of the block with a paintbrush.

4 Press the block onto a rectangle of heavy paper. Apply pressure evenly to ensure good contact with the paper. Carefully remove the block, taking care not to smudge the paint. When the bookplate has dried, trim the paper to size.

Bookmarks

Don't lose your place! Remember where you are with these jolly bookmarks. They fit neatly over the top of the page so that you don't have to leaf through your book every time you want to catch up on some reading.

YOU WILL NEED
heavy purple and yellow paper
pencil
scissors
scraps of thin coloured paper
non-toxic paper glue

paper glue

scissors   *pencil*

paper

1 Draw a bird shape on the heavy purple paper and cut it out.

2 Draw the bird's beak, legs, wings and front onto appropriately coloured pieces of paper. Cut them out.

3 Stick the coloured details onto the front of the bird with paper glue.

4 Cut the giraffe bookmark from heavy yellow paper. Cut spots from orange paper and additional features from appropriately coloured scraps and stick them in place.

Papier-mâché Necklace

Papier-mâché is made by recycling old paper and cardboard; why not carry on this ecological theme by decorating a papier-mâché necklace with daisies and insects – you'll blend in well at any garden party!

YOU WILL NEED
large coin, for tracing circles
corrugated cardboard
pencil
scissors
newspaper
diluted non-toxic PVA (white) glue
non-toxic white paint
paintbrush
non-toxic paint in a variety of colours
non-toxic clear gloss varnish
darning needle
non-toxic strong glue
eye pins
coloured cord

paint

paintbrush

strong glue

scissors

needle

eye pins

pencil

cardboard

newspaper

cord

1 Place a round object such as a coin on the cardboard. Draw around it to make 12 discs and cut them out.

2 Cover each disc with three layers of thin papier-mâché strips. Leave them to dry overnight.

3 Prime each disc with two coats of white paint and leave to dry.

4 Draw a daisy or ladybird (ladybug) on each disc. Fill in the design with paints.

5 Seal each disc with two coats of gloss varnish. When they are dry, with adult help, make a hole in the top of each with a darning needle. Dab a little strong glue over each hole and push in an eye pin.

6 Cut a length of cord. Pass the cord through the eye pin of each disc and tie it before adding the next.

Papier-mâché Earrings

These earrings would make a good gift, and the beauty of papier-mâché is that however large the earrings, they won't weigh your ears down!

YOU WILL NEED
tracing paper
pencil
corrugated cardboard
scissors
newspaper
diluted non-toxic PVA (white) glue
fine sandpaper
non-toxic white paint
paintbrush
non-toxic paint in a variety of colours
non-toxic clear gloss varnish
darning needle
non-toxic strong glue
pair of eye pins
pliers
earring clips

paintbrush

paint

strong glue

earring clips

scissors

eye pins

cardboard

pencil

needle

tracing paper

newspaper

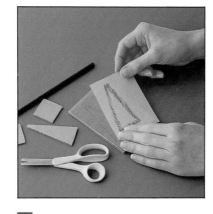

1 Trace the earring pieces from the template and transfer them to the cardboard twice. Cut them out.

2 Cover all the earring pieces in three layers of thin papier-mâché strips. Allow them to dry overnight.

3 Smooth the earring pieces with sandpaper, then prime with two coats of white paint and leave to dry.

4 Decorate the earring pieces with bright paints and leave to dry.

5 Seal the dry earring pieces with two coats of gloss varnish.

6 With adult help, make a small hole in each piece with the darning needle. Dab a little strong glue over each hole and push an eye pin into each. Leave the glue to dry. With adult help, use pliers to open the loops of the eye pins in the lower half of each earring. Hook the lower to the upper half, and close the loops. Use strong glue to attach the earring clips and allow to dry thoroughly.

Papier-mâché Brooch

Animal designs make good brooches; you could also make earrings to match these two jolly creatures. The brooch backs are known as 'findings' and can be bought from craft, hobby and jewellery shops.

YOU WILL NEED
tracing paper
pencil
corrugated cardboard
scissors
newspaper
diluted non-toxic PVA (white) glue
fine sandpaper
paintbrush
non-toxic white paint
non-toxic paint in a variety of
    colours
non-toxic clear gloss varnish
brooch fastening
non-toxic strong glue

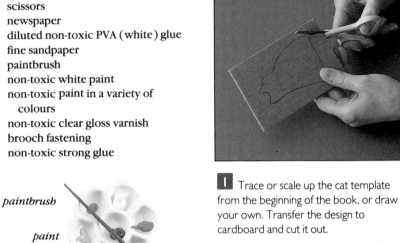

paintbrush

paint

strong glue

sandpaper

scissors

cardboard

pencil

tracing paper

brooch fastening

newspaper

1 Trace or scale up the cat template from the beginning of the book, or draw your own. Transfer the design to cardboard and cut it out.

2 Cover the cat with three layers of thin papier-mâché strips. Allow to dry thoroughly.

3 Smooth the surface of the brooch with fine sandpaper, then paint it white and leave to dry.

4 Draw in the cat's features, and then decorate the brooch with paint.

5 When the paint is thoroughly dry, seal the brooch with two coats of gloss varnish. Leave to dry.

6 Attach a brooch fastening to the back of the cat with strong glue. Let the brooch dry overnight before you wear it. Other designs of your choice may be made in the same way.

Stationery Folder in Fancy Paper

These folders would make welcome presents for an avid correspondent. They can be labelled by subject or name to make a useful filing system.

YOU WILL NEED
decorative paper
ruler
pencil
scissors
non-toxic paper glue

scissors

paper glue

ruler

pencil

paper

1 On the wrong side of the decorative paper measure and draw a rectangle 32 × 47 cm (12½ × 18½ in). Cut it out.

2 Following the template at the beginning of the book, mark out the folder on the wrong side of the rectangle of paper.

3 Cut out the top notch and flap from the folder.

4 Fold the side panels to the centre of the folder and stick them together. Fold the bottom flap over the side panels and stick it in place.

Letter File

Important and treasured letters should be saved, and a letter file is the perfect container. Illustrate yours with colourful cut-outs for a stylish effect.

YOU WILL NEED
heavy paper
ruler
pencil
scissors
non-toxic paper glue
scraps of thin coloured paper

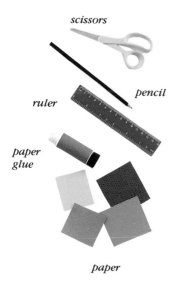

scissors

pencil

ruler

paper glue

paper

1 Measure and draw a rectangle 47 × 32 cm (18½ × 12½ in) on heavy coloured paper. Cut it out.

2 Following the diagram, mark up the rectangle to form the file. Cut away the excess paper and stick the side panels together in the centre. Stick the base flap over the bottom of the side panels.

3 Cut out a hand motif from red paper. Cut an asymmetrical rectangle from blue paper to represent an envelope. Cut the stamp from yellow and orange scraps.

4 Carefully stick the cut-outs to the front of the letter file. You can make additional files in the same way, decorated with your own designs.

Foil-covered Frame

Do you have a favourite photograph or picture that deserves a special frame? Why not make one in papier-mâché? This one looks very impressive with its colourful foil surface and will take standard-sized photographs.

YOU WILL NEED
graph paper
thick and thin corrugated cardboard
pencil
ruler
scissors
non-toxic strong glue
newspaper
diluted non-toxic PVA (white) glue
paintbrush
non-toxic white paint
silver foil
coloured foil
2 picture hangers
thin cord

coloured foil

silver foil *cardboard*

scissors *strong glue* *cord*

pencil

newspaper

ruler

1 Scale up each piece of frame from the template at the beginning of the book onto appropriate cardboard. The front and back frame should be drawn onto thick cardboard, and the spacer on thin. Cut out each piece.

2 Stick the spacer to the frame front with strong glue.

3 Cover both sections with three layers of papier-mâché strips. Allow the frame to dry overnight in a warm place.

4 Prime the dry frame pieces with white paint. Although the paint won't be seen it will be easier to see where to stick the foil if the surface of the frame is white.

5 Cover the frame pieces with silver foil. Stick the frame front to the back. Cover the joins with strips of foil.

6 Cut small circles of coloured foil and stick them around the frame. Stick the hangers to the back of the frame with strong glue, and add the cord to hang the frame.

Papier-mâché Mirror Frame

This twinkling mirror frame will create a sparkling focal point in any room. It is decorated with a variety of interesting sequins, but other objects such as colourful buttons, bottle tops and small shaped buttons would be just as good.

YOU WILL NEED
tracing paper or graph paper
corrugated cardboard
pencil
ruler
scissors
masking tape
2 picture hangers
newspaper
diluted non-toxic PVA (white) glue
paintbrush
non-toxic white paint
non-toxic bright paint
non-toxic strong glue
sequins
non-toxic clear gloss varnish
12 × 12 cm (4¾ × 4¾ in) mirror tile
thin cord

1 Trace or scale up the mirror frame pieces from the template at the beginning of the book and transfer to heavy cardboard. Cut them out.

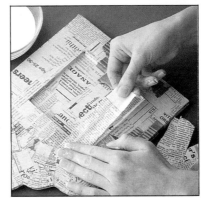

2 Use masking tape to stick the front and back of the frame together. Stick the hangers to the frame back with small pieces of masking tape.

3 Cover the entire frame with three layers of papier-mâché, avoiding the metal hangers. Leave the frame to dry overnight in a warm place.

4 Prime the frame with two coats of white paint. Leave to dry.

sequins   paintbrush

mirror tile   paint

scissors

picture hangers   cardboard

strong glue   cord

ruler   pencil   masking tape

newspaper

5 Give the frame two coats of bright paint and let it dry thoroughly. Stick the sequins around the frame. Varnish the frame with a coat of clear varnish.

6 Stick the mirror tile in place. Tie a cord through the metal hangers on the back of the frame.

INDEX

A

Album, photograph, 75

B

Beads, rolled paper, 71
Bird mosaic tray, 22
Bookmarks, 83
Bookplates, 82
Brooch, papier-mâché, 88

C

Calendar, 31
Cardboard, 8
    corrugated, 8
Cards, woven paper, 28
Cat paper cut picture, 70
Christmas decorations, 33
    papier-mâché, 36
Christmas wreath, 34
Coloured paper, 8
Cork place mats, 38
Corrugated card, 8
Corrugated gift tags, 78
Cotton string, 10
Cowboy face mask, 54
Crayons, 10
Crêpe paper, 8
Crocodile, 45
Crowns, 56
Curling, 13
Cutting, 13

D

Decorated corrugated card, 8
Decorations, Christmas, 33
    papier-mâché, 36
Decoupage frame, 26
Doll, dressing-up, 46
Doll's house paper, 8
Dotty notebook, 58
Dressing-up doll, 46

E

Earrings, papier-mâché, 86
Equipment, 10
Eye masks, 52
Eye pins, 10

F

Fancy wrapped parcels, 80
Finger puppets, 60
Flowers, paper, 72
Foam rubber stamps,
    printing with, 16
Foil-covered frame, 92
Fold-out greetings card, 75
Folding, 12

Frame
    foil-covered, 92
    mirror, papier-mâché, 94
Frieze, stencilled, 40

G

Games
    jigsaw, 68
    magnetic fish game, 61
    noughts and crosses, 64
    snap, 55
    Tic-Tac-Toe, 64
Garden hat, 66
Gift tags
    corrugated, 78
    paper, 79
Glue
    paper, 10
    PVA, 10
    strong, 10
    white, 10
Graph paper, 8
Greetings cards
    fold-out, 75
    recycled paper, 74

H

Handmade paper, 8
Hat, garden, 66
Hole punch, 10
Horse, stained glass, 42
Horse tableau, 62
Household sponge, 10

I

Ink pad, 10

J

Jigsaw, 68

L

Letter file, 91

M

Magnetic fish game, 61
Masking tape, 10
Masks
    cowboy face, 54
    eye, 52
    sun and moon, 51
Materials, 10
Mirror frame,
    papier-mâché, 94
Mobile, space, 48
Monocle disguise, 50
Monster feet, 44
Moon mask, 51

N

Necklace, papier-mâché, 84
Notebook, dotty, 58
Noughts and crosses, 64

O

Origami paper, 8

P

Paintbrushes, 10
Painted postcards, 24
Paints, 10
Paper
    coloured, 8
    crêpe, 8
    doll's house, 8
    graph, 8
    handmade, 8
    origami, 8
    recycled, 8
    tissue, 8
    tracing, 8
Paper chains, 32
Paper clips, 10
Paper fasteners, 10
Paper flowers, 72
Paper gift tags, 79
Paper glue, 10
Paper ribbon, 8
Papercuts
    cat picture, 70
Papier-mâché, 14
    brooch, 88
    Christmas decorations, 36
    earrings, 86

mirror frame, 94
    necklace, 84
Parcels, fancy wrapped, 80
Pencils, coloured, 10
Photograph album, 76
Photograph frame, foil-covered,
    94
Picture
    cat papercut, 70
Place mats, cork, 38
Postcards
    calendar, 31
    painted, 24
Posterboard
    corrugated, 8
    thin, 8
Printed wrapping paper, 25
Printing
    foam rubber stamps, with, 16
Puppets, finger, 60
PVA glue, 10

R

Recycled paper, 8
Recycled paper greetings cards,
    74
Ribbon, paper, 8
Rolled paper beads, 71
Rubber cutting mat, 10
Rubber-stamped stationery, 39
Ruler, 10

S

Scaling-up, 17
Scissors, 10
Scoring, 12
Sequins, 10
Snap cards, stencilled, 55
Space mobile, 48
Spinner, 30
Sponging, 16
Stained-glass horse, 42
Stapler and staples, 10
Stationery holder, fancy paper, 90
Stationery, rubber-stamped, 39
Stencil board, 8
Stencilling, 15
    frieze, 40
    snap cards, 55
Sticky tape, 10
Strong glue, 10
Sun and moon masks, 51

T

Templates, 18–21
Thin board, 8
Tic-Tac-Toe, 64
Tissue paper, 8
Tracing, 17
Tracing paper, 8
Tray, bird mosaic, 22

W

White glue, 10
Woven paper cards, 28
Wrapping paper, printed, 25
Wreath, Christmas, 34

ACKNOWLEDGEMENTS

The author would like to thank James Duncan for taking such great
photographs; Lucy Sykes for appearing in the book; Madeleine Brehaut
for kindly letting us raid her props; and Lindsay Porter for her help
styling the finished pictures.